Love, Life, Loss, and Other Findings

Nicole Rheinhardt

BookLeaf Publishing

Presentation by *BookLeaf Publishing*

Web: www.bookleafpub.com

E-mail: info@bookleafpub.com

ISBN: 9789357210010

First edition 2022

DEDICATION

To my mother, she is my soul.

To my father, he was my heart.

And to my mind, for it is my salvation.

Origin

There is hurt
Here,
Crashing in on rocky shores.

Memories drift in like morning fog
Turning the air to licorice
Thick and sour
Swept in by the mundane
Pushed back out to sea

A city in California
The landmark signs of home
Now read like a tombstone

A lifetime of searching
For an explanation
For an answer

But I know that people are rarely ever answers

Galaxies
Crafted
In that one-bedroom apartment
Exist as ruins now
Hollow
They whisper

Through hallways in my mind
Like unspoken secrets

What you took
I cannot replace
You didn't just remove yourself
You removed pieces of me
I didn't realize were wrapped in you

My heart tainted with hatred
A high tide
Of disappointment and sorrow

Wondering who it this makes you
Who it makes me

An ocean of burden to carry
It would have been lighter to carry you,
Wounded and broken,
Easier to shift under your turmoil
Than to stand firm under the weight of these waves.

Where You're Planted

You aim to pick fights.
The while I'm bathed
In a new laughter,
Baptized queen
With no need for anything
More than an authentic self.

Turns out you were right,
We are not compatible.

Because I was the cherry blossom
Longing for spring
To bloom.

And you were like tree rot,
All-consuming
Weakening me from the knees.

How could fragility
Love decay
And hope for eternity?

Unsighted

I excused your claws
And defended your fangs
But it wasn't the mob,
Pitchforks in tow,
Who were blind.

It was me,
For not seeing the beast
You had become.

Hindsight

If I knew
What I know now
Oh, the choices
I'd make differently.

But I am choosing
Now
To forgive myself.

I was working with the puzzle pieces
I had at the time
Unable to see the full picture.

Free Vacation

If time had stopped
For just a day
And we could move
Through the chaos
With ease
How would we waste the hours?

Whisper
Your shenanigans in my ear
Drum them into my mind

Let the humming
Of anxious worries
Drown
In your velvet bourbon voice
Just long enough for me to drift
Far away from here

If Only...

Echoing in the distance:
My naivety
Fuels delusions
Of your return.

I see you
Hiding
If only two cars behind me,
Afraid to approach.

I'm sure you're still
Piecing together
The explanation
That beckons my forgiveness.

You'll need one
To erase this time apart.

So I'll keep looking,
Around corners and alleyways
For a glimpse of you,
A shadow,
A mirage.

If only to keep my peace,

My hope,
My drive.
You owe me that much.

If only you were there.
If only the delusion didn't have to die.
And my imagination could
Run wild with impossible grandeur...

If only for my sake.

The Last Word

She was thirty-five,
If a day.
She had in mind,
A totally different person;
A sort of semi-mystical man.

He was an expert,
At cutting corners.
And when there were no corners left,
He would make circles rounder.

Love –
She withdrew –
should be a by-product
of living and worship,
rather than its own end.

But as if on the wings of the wind,
He had disappeared.

She laid the envelope on the table.
The world snowed on her.
This is her weakness.

And occasionally,

His eyes fell,
On the manila envelope.
But he never opened it.

Starry Night

At the end of the day,
We are all just a small spec
Of insignificant creatures
Laying on a marble.

Our hair spilling onto the lap of gravity,
Looking upside down
At infinite universes.

Lighting the skies,
Sprinkled into the celestial blue
Outskirts of the cosmos
That lay just beyond the horizon,
The all-seeing moon,
Peeks through the twilight,
Rippling the skies into obscure shades of sapphire
To guide us all home.

Woman

Woman,
Who came from man's rib
Yet is still required to be his backbone.
Woman,
Who is burdened with the blood of a mistake she never made
Woman,
Who is planned for perfection
In an imperfect world
Woman,
Who adjusts her oh-so-perfect curves
To fit the mold that man has made for her.
Woman,
Who has bowed down to these expectations
Willingly
I say to you,
You
Are woman,
Portal from this world to the preceding.
You force beauty out of something un-neat and messy.
You confine yourself to cotton cages that promise to
"Perk" here
"Lift" there

as if your head is not already held high.

You were made to believe your body was cursed
That this punishable form had to be protected
From those who would try to take you
You were never taught
That you shouldn't have to worry about being taken,
That the sound of the words “I love you”
Should be more familiar
Than the sight of you undressing

You were made to feel broken
As if your emotional state
Has direct correlation with your time of the month

But menstruation doesn’t cause frustration
The anger comes from the expectations
To be pretty
To be smart
Willing to open my legs whenever you ask
As if I’m still a virgin because no one has ever asked!

We were taught to be precious
Like porcelain dolls
We were taught to sit on the shelf
And speak only when spoken to

But my voice has outgrown my mouth
Since the day I was born
I knew I was
Woman
And that meant I was strong

My Love

If I gave you what you wanted
You'd refund it
Everyone always does
Perhaps it was too much
Or not enough...

Like honey
It will melt in your palms
Stick to you until
You wash yourself of me

In the Wake

After you died
A younger version of me
Approached
Asked “Does this mean we start waiting again?”
You see she is used to waiting for you

She remembers the months of separation
Until the summer heat joined
The two of you together

I wept for her
She spent many nights
Wishing away tears
And praying you’d stay

I, however, know better
I know that every night
Will be filled with the ache
Of waiting
And the scorch of summer
Won’t be enough to mend
The breaking of my heart

I held her close
“Yes, we will have to keep waiting...”

Tears racing down my cheek
“This time we’ll wait together.”

Un-educating

You silenced me
Uninterested
When my passionate lips
Filled my cup to the brim

You shamed me
When my anxiety
Swelled
Crept up inside me
And stuffed me in a lead box

I made myself
Small
For you
Muzzled my mind
And anchored my fears
To please you

And often I forget
The shackles have fallen

I pause
To remind myself
There are those who will listen
Ungrudgingly

So I will move
Onward
Like a river
Bursting through a dam
You will no longer prevent me
From moving along
My natural path

For all the years I learned to accommodate you
I am unlearning

[Severely Untitled]

Starry conversations with you
Mirror exchanges between me and myself
My heart and my mind
You've taken residence in my head
An ocean-view suite
Giving perspective to my inner self

Typical of me
To disguise as a bank vault
But you weren't fooled
Saw the trap door
And waltzed inside

Unlike past burglars,
Didn't take what was there
Instead, you left pieces of you.
Added to its collective value
And told me
"This is how it should be."

Blank Page

This blank page
Mocks me
Promises me potential
Fills me with hope
And often disappoints

This blank page and I
Quarrel daily

Is it too much to ask
This blank page
To deliver on its end of the bargain?

Sitting there
Rigidly stern
Margins like corral gates.
Do you feel no responsibility
For the atrocities you allow me to write?

Denouement

I often wonder if I should call
Or maybe send a text.
Have you, too, been secretly waiting
Or have you already found what's next?

Perhaps it wasn't obvious
And maybe I didn't say,
But I miss you tremendously -
More and more every day.

The comfort of your laugh;
The smell of your embrace;
In the mornings, rolling over
Just to see your face.

Would anything change
If I spoke from my heart?
Would it do more damage?
Cause your peace to depart?

I left to make you happy
Killing myself along the drive.
Holding onto the hope
That our love would still survive.

I see now that you're content
Making your like anew
While I grip tightly
To memories of you

Thinking of our first encounter
Savoring every bite
The sway of our conversations
That led into the night

I know we weren't perfect
We didn't always get it right
But even after all this hurting
For you, I'd always fight

So should I break the silence?
Give us another try?
Or am I making it harder
To say the final goodbye?

Your actions speak your answer
You're ready to cut the tie
And I should let you go
Let this love of mine die

But let this poem be a testament
To my feelings through and through
Because I desperately hate rhyming
But I'm doing it for you

Color Theory

My childhood
Vibrantly tinted
In flushes of blue and violet

Later years
Pioneered a deep turquoise
Of melancholy and manipulation

And for a while
This was the world
A spectrum of cool pigments
Flashing through my mind

Enter you

And my mind glowed yellow
Cheeks rang red
And the world felt like it would never be the
same

Silver Lining

While you continuously piss me off,
This hate
Is great kindling
For the flames of my art.

Countenance

May you find
A laugh
To fill your lungs
Thrash your head back
And pinch your hips

May you find
A passion
To motivate your sunrises
And satisfy your sunsets

May you have days
Filled with blissful nothingness

May your successes
Be bountiful
And deserving of your labor

May the life you live
Be of your creation

May love find you
Unexpectedly
And may you be ready to open the door
When it does

A Low Whisper

One day I'll find the response
To all of those prayers.

Someone unafraid of forever
Capable of pulling the moon from the sky
Starstruck by my light
And humbled by my love

All the fighting
And lessons learned
Will become steady preparation
For the blessing
That has always been
At the end of that long, dark tunnel.

I will hear His voice
A low whisper
Of reassurance
"This is what I have given you"

My Garden

"No weapon that is formed against thee shall prosper..."

The swords you cast to kill me
I will transform
To shovels and rakes
To tend to my garden.

I will flourish.
And spring will bring new life
To what was once desolate.

Finale

At least
This hurt,
However devastating,
Is the last opportunity
They have.

www.ingramcontent.com/pod-product-compliance
Lightning Source LLC
Chambersburg PA
CBHW051754130826
49812CB00033B/1148